FOSSILS

Megan Lappi

MEDIA ENHANCED BOOKS
AV2 BY WEIGL
ADDED VALUE · AUDIO VISUAL

www.av2books.com

BOOK CODE

H318392

AV² by Weigl brings you media enhanced books that support active learning.

AV² provides enriched content that supplements and complements this book. Weigl's AV² books strive to create inspired learning and engage young minds for a total learning experience.

Go to **www.av2books.com**, and enter this book's unique code. You will have access to video, audio, web links, quizzes, a slide show, and activities.

Audio
Listen to sections of the book read aloud.

Video
Watch informative video clips.

Web Link
Find research sites and play interactive games.

Try This!
Complete activities and hands-on experiments.

Due to the dynamic nature of the Internet, some of the URLs and activities provided as part of AV² by Weigl may have changed or ceased to exist. AV² by Weigl accepts no responsibility for any such changes. All media enhanced books are regularly monitored to update addresses and sites in a timely manner. Contact AV² by Weigl at 1-866-649-3445 or av2books@weigl.com with any questions, comments, or feedback.

Published by AV² by Weigl
350 5th Avenue, 59th Floor
New York, NY 10118
Website: www.av2books.com   www.weigl.com

Library of Congress Cataloging-in-Publication Data

Lappi, Megan.
 Fossils / Megan Lappi.
    p. cm.
 Includes index.
 ISBN 978-1-60596-973-2 (hardcover : alk. paper) -- ISBN 978-1-60596-974-9 (softcover : alk. paper) -- ISBN 978-1-60596-975-6 (e-book)
1. Fossils--Juvenile literature. I. Title.
 QE714.5.L3572 2010
 560--dc22
                          2009050237

Printed in the United States of America in North Mankato, Minnesota
1 2 3 4 5 6 7 8 9 0 14 13 12 11 10

052010
WEP264000

Project Coordinator: Heather C. Hudak
Design: Terry Paulhus

Photo Credits
Weigl acknowledges Getty Images as its primary image supplier for this title.

Every reasonable effort has been made to trace ownership and to obtain permission to reprint copyright material. The publishers would be pleased to have any errors or omissions brought to their attention so that they may be corrected in subsequent printings.

CONTENTS

Coal is a type of fossil. Most of the coal used today is the remains of vast swamps and forests that covered Earth more than 300 million years ago. Today, coal is the most common fuel on Earth for making electricity. When coal is burned, it produces carbon dioxide, as well as many harmful chemicals. Reducing the amount of coal used is important to having a healthy environment in the future. Saving energy at home by making sure that lights and appliances are turned off when they are not being used can help reduce the need for coal.

Studying Fossils

Fossils are the rocklike remains of ancient animals and plants. A fossil can be a hard part of an animal, such as a shell or a tooth. It can also be a footprint left behind in the mud. Fossils are usually found in layered rock called sedimentary rock. Each layer of rock, deeper than the last, contains material from a earlier age. The word fossil comes from the Latin word *fossilis*, which means "dug up."

Millions of plant and animal **species** have lived on Earth during the past three billion years. Many of these species, such as dinosaurs, are now **extinct**. Paleontologists study fossils to learn about creatures and plants that lived in the past. Fossils tell when and how these plants and animals lived. However, fossils have not been found for many species. Scientists may never find fossils for some species.

Fossils of some dinosaurs, such as Albertosaurus, are very rare. The few that have been found teach scientists a great deal about how these animals lived.

■ Skull fossils help scientists learn how dinosaurs heard, saw, smelled, and ate. Footprint fossils tell scientists how fast dinosaurs ran.

Fossil Formation

Most animals and plants do not become fossils. Many of them rot. Others are eaten by **scavengers**. A fossil forms when a plant or the body of a dead animal is covered by mud or sand. Over time, **sediment** covers the body or plant. After thousands of years, it becomes a fossil. Fossils continue to form every day. Future scientists will find the fossils that are forming today.

The Process of Forming a Fossil

This diagram shows what happens to an animal's body after it dies. If the conditions are suitable, the animal's remains will become fossilized.

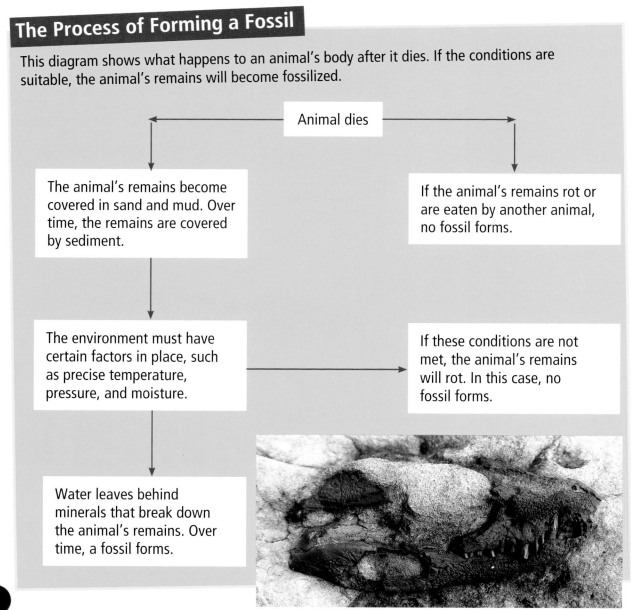

Animal dies

The animal's remains become covered in sand and mud. Over time, the remains are covered by sediment.

If the animal's remains rot or are eaten by another animal, no fossil forms.

The environment must have certain factors in place, such as precise temperature, pressure, and moisture.

If these conditions are not met, the animal's remains will rot. In this case, no fossil forms.

Water leaves behind minerals that break down the animal's remains. Over time, a fossil forms.

Scientists have found many sea creature fossils. This is because sediment is usually deposited, or laid down, in the ocean.

Fossils can form in many ways. The remains of a plant or animal may be replaced by **minerals**. They may be dissolved over time so that only an **impression** remains.

Many fossils become stone. This happens when water enters a plant's or animal's remains. Over time, the water breaks down the remains and leaves minerals behind. Slowly, the entire shape of the remains are replaced with minerals. The plant or animal remains appear to have turned to stone. Petrified Forest National Park in Arizona has many trees that have become stone.

■ Arizona's Petrified Forest National Park contains fossils that are 225 million years old.

Amber and Footprints

Not all plants and animals become stone fossils. Sometimes, a whole plant or animal is **preserved**. Then, scientists see exactly what the plant or animal looked like when it was alive. Millions of years ago, sticky sap oozed from pine tree stems, just as it does today. Sometimes, an insect or plant seed became stuck in the sap. Over time, the sap hardened and became another type of fossil called amber.

Amber is yellow and looks like glass. Today, people make jewelry out of amber. Amber pieces with fossils of insects or seeds inside them are valuable.

■ Most amber is mined. Lumps of amber weighing up to 18 pounds (8 kilograms) have been found.

Footprints left in mud are called trace fossils. Trace fossils are more common than fossils of an entire body. One animal can leave thousands of traces behind. These fossils tell scientists how fast an animal moved. Trace fossils tell the animal's height and weight, too. Very large animal footprints are spaced far apart. Small animal footprints are close together. If many animal footprints are found together, scientists know that the animals lived together in **herds**.

The smallest dinosaur footprint found was only 1 inch (2.5 centimeters) long. The footprint was likely made by an animal about the size of a sparrow.

Make Your Own Footprint

Have you ever thought about making your own footprint? Try the experiment below to create your very own trace fossil.

Step 1
Find a piece of clay. Place the clay on a piece of cardboard. Then, smooth and flatten the clay using a rolling pin. The clay should be about 2 inches (5 cm) thick.

Step 2
Take off your shoe and sock. Press your bare foot into the clay to make a footprint. Now, set the clay aside to harden.

Step 3
After a few days, the clay will be as hard as stone. One day, it will be a fossil.

Fossils Over Time

Scientists have divided Earth's history into blocks of time called eras. Different types of animals lived during each era.

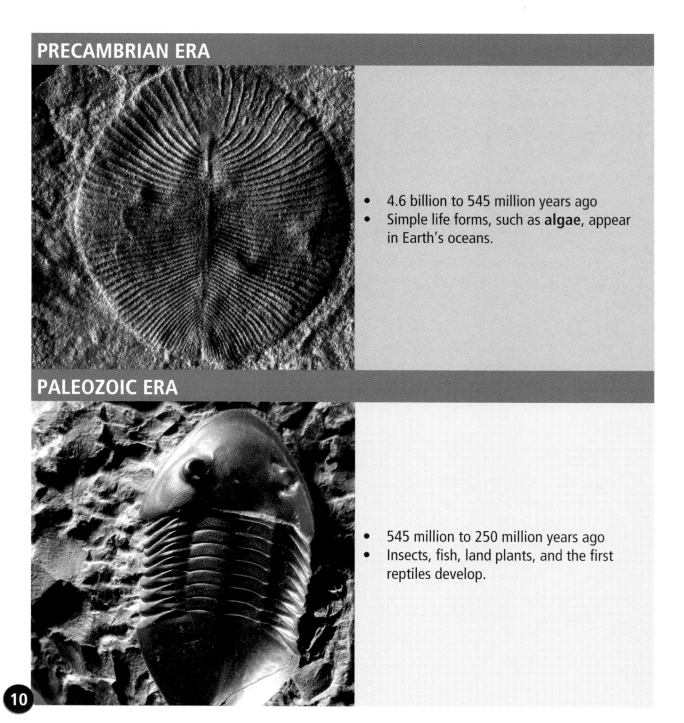

PRECAMBRIAN ERA

- 4.6 billion to 545 million years ago
- Simple life forms, such as **algae**, appear in Earth's oceans.

PALEOZOIC ERA

- 545 million to 250 million years ago
- Insects, fish, land plants, and the first reptiles develop.

Fossils form in layers of rock. Scientists can tell which eras animals lived in from the layer of rock that contains the fossils. Fossils found in upper layers are younger than fossils found in lower layers.

MESOZOIC ERA

- 250 million to 65 million years ago
- Dinosaurs and birds develop from earlier life forms.
- The era is also known as the "Age of Reptiles."

CENOZOIC ERA

- 65 million years ago to present
- All types of **mammals**, including humans, develop during this era.
- The era is also called the "Age of Mammals."

Fossils Around the World

ARCTIC
OCEAN

NORTH
AMERICA

Smilodon
(Saber-Toothed Cat)
Location: North America
Country: United States
Fast Fact: This animal went extinct about 11,700 years ago. It was a little smaller than a lion and had a skull that was 12 inches (30 cm) long.

PACIFIC
OCEAN

ATLANTIC
OCEAN

Triceratops
Location: North America
Country: United States
Fast Fact: Often, Triceratops skulls have scars. Triceratops most likely fought each other to be leader.

SOUTH
AMERICA

Tyrannosaurus Rex
Location: North America
Country: United States
Fast Fact: The largest, most complete, Tyrannosaurus Rex fossil ever found is 42 feet (12.8 meters) long. The Tyrannosaurus Rex was one of the biggest land based meat eaters ever.

N
W E
S

621 Miles
0   1,000 Kilometers

Legend
★ Location of fossil finds

This map shows the location of certain fossil finds around the world.
Research online to answer these questions.
1. Where have the largest numbers of fossils been found?
2. What are some recent fossil finds?

**ARCTIC
OCEAN**

EUROPE

Pliosaur
Location: Europe
Country: United Kingdom
Fast Fact: These "sea monsters"
are thought to have been between 16
and 85 feet (5 and 25 meters) long. This
is three times the size of a killer whale.

**PACIFIC
OCEAN**

AFRICA

**INDIAN
OCEAN**

AUSTRALIA

**SOUTHERN
OCEAN**

Dinosaur Footprints
Location: Australia
Country: Australia
Fast Fact: In Queensland, there
are 3,300 fossilized dinosaur footprints. These
footprints came from about 150 dinosaurs.

ANTARCTICA

The Great Bone Rush

The first dinosaur bones were found in the 1820s in England. At first, people did not know what they had found. Soon, they realized that reptile-like creatures must have once lived on Earth. In 1842, British scientist Sir Richard Owen called these creatures *Dinosauria*, which means "terrible lizards."

In the 1870s, the "Bone Wars" began in the United States. Two men, Othniel Charles Marsh and Edward Drinker Cope, competed to find fossils. To get the fossils to museums quickly, the two men covered the fossils in plaster.

■ Paleontologists study fossilized animal droppings called coprolites. This helps them understand what dinosaurs ate.

Many fossilized plants and animals are extinct, meaning none of them are alive today. Most extinctions happen when the environment changes, and animals cannot adapt fast enough to survive. Today, the huge changes humans are making to the environment are causing many species to become extinct. These extinctions are happening up to a 1,000 times faster than in the past. By working to preserve sensitive areas, such as wetlands, people can help protect species from extinction.

Fossils Through History

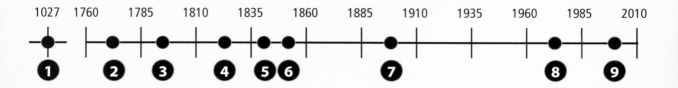

1027 1760 1785 1810 1835 1860 1885 1910 1935 1960 1985 2010

1 2 3 4 5 6 7 8 9

1 **1027**
Avicenna, a scientist living in what is today called Iraq, first suggests that fossils might be formed by mineral-rich fluids.

2 **1770**
Giant fossil bones are found in the Netherlands.

3 **1795**
Georges Cuvier, a French scientist, identifies the bones found in the Netherlands. They belong to an extinct swimming dinosaur called a mosasaur.

4 **1823**
Human bones are found with bones from a woolly mammoth. This is evidence that humans and mammoths lived at the same time.

5 **1842**
Sir Richard Owen of England creates the word "dinosauria" to describe the fossils of giant reptiles.

6 **1855**
The fossil of a feathered dinosaur, archaeopteryx, is found in Germany.

7 **1909**
The Burgess Shale is discovered. This fossil bed contains some of the earliest **multi-cellular** life forms.

8 **1974**
Donald Johanson discovers a fossil that is nearly 3.2 million years old. The fossil, which is closely related to humans, is named "Lucy."

9 **2004**
The 375-million-year-old fossil of a *Tiktaalik roseae* is discovered in the Canadian arctic. The creature was an early amphibian.

Dinosaur Detectives

Paleontologists study fossils to understand the types of life that were on Earth millions of years ago. Some paleontologists search for fossils. Once a fossil is discovered, it is the job of a paleontologist to remove the fossil from the ground. The fossil is then sent to a laboratory to be studied.

Digging up a fossil is difficult. Paleontologists must be careful not to damage the fossil. First, paleontologists use small tools to clear away the rock or earth around the fossil. Then photographs are taken and pictures are drawn of where the fossil was found. Paleontologists study these images later.

If a fossil is surrounded by soft material, such as clay, it is wrapped in layers of cloth dipped in plaster. When the plaster sets, the fossil is turned over. Then the other side is plastered. Each fossil is labeled, so the scientists in the laboratory know what it is and where it was found.

■ Some fossilized animals have living relatives today. Dragonflies that are preserved as fossils appear very similar to dragonflies that live today.

Once the fossilized pieces of an animal or plant are at the laboratory, paleontologists remove the plaster jackets. They use power tools to carefully remove rock from each fossil. Once all the rock is removed, the fossilized pieces are glued together.

The pieces are very heavy, so a copy is often made using molds of the original bones. A steel framework is built, and the bones are connected together.

■ Complete fossilized skeletons are often displayed in museums.

What Did Dinosaurs Look Like?

Paleontologists know what the skin of some dinosaurs looked like. This is because they have found fossilized impressions of dinosaur skin.

Paleontologists have no way of knowing the dinosaur's skin color. However, some scientists believe dinosaurs had good eyesight. This may mean their skin was brightly colored so other dinosaurs could see them.

Meat-eating dinosaurs may have had spots or stripes like a leopard or a tiger. Plant-eating dinosaurs may have been **camouflaged** to hide from **predators** such as Tyrannosaurus rex. Scientists may never know exactly how dinosaurs looked.

■ Scientists believe Tyrannosaurus rex could eat about 500 pounds (227 kilograms) in one bite.

Becoming a Paleontologist

Are you interested in studying fossils for a living? Consider the following factors to help decide if paleontology is a career you would like to pursue.

Paleontologists are interested in science and often are curious and patient. In high school, they often show their interest by studying biology and math. They then go to university, where many future paleontogists earn degrees in geology or zoology.

Barnum Brown

Barnum Brown was one of the greatest fossil hunters of the 20th century. He was a paleontologist for 66 years. Brown traveled all over the world collecting dinosaur and mammal fossils. He was the first person to discover the bones of a fierce meat-eating dinosaur. Later, Henry Fairfield Osborn named the dinosaur Tyrannosaurus rex.

Pick

Working Conditions
Paleontologists often work outdoors, digging for fossils. They are sometimes required to travel. Paleontologists also spend time in laboratories studying fossils.

Seven Facts About Fossils

Fossils date back billions of years. The oldest fossil ever found is 3.5 billion years old.

Hard objects, such as bones, shells, and teeth, do not break down as easily as the rest of an animal's body. For this reason, they are common fossils.

Scientists can study details about a dinosaur's life by studying fossils.

Dinosaur fossils have been discovered on every continent.

A fossil is more like a rock than the animal it once was.

Imprints of feathers have been found in some dinosaur fossils. This could mean that some dinosaurs are related to birds.

Sauroposeidon is the biggest dinosaur fossil ever found. This dinosaur is thought to have weighed as much as eight elephants.

Fossil Brain Teasers

1 Are the dinosaurs in museums real fossils or copies?

2 In which era did dinosaurs live?

3 Can tree sap form fossils?

4 What can turn into a fossil?

5 What is a trace fossil?

6 When were fossils first discovered?

7 In what kind of rocks are fossils often found?

8 What can paleontologists learn by studying coprolites?

9 Which famous paleontologist discovered Tyrannosaurus rex?

10 What does "fossil" mean in Latin?

ANSWERS: 1. Most dinosaurs in museum displays are copies of fossils, made from lightweight materials. **2.** The Mesozoic Era **3.** Yes. Insects and plant seeds can be preserved as fossils in hardened tree sap called amber. **4.** Almost any living thing. Plants, animals, and even bacteria can all turn into fossils. **5.** A trace fossil shows how big and heavy the animal was. An example is a dinosaur footprint. **6.** Fossils were first discovered in the 1820s. **7.** sedimentary rock **8.** Coprolites tell paleontologists what an animal ate. **9.** Barnum Brown **10.** dug up

Make Your Own Fossil

A fossil can be made from something as simple as a leaf found in your backyard.

Tools Needed

Small pail

Leaves or shells

Soil

Water

Spoon

Baking Pan

Directions

1 Mix water and soil in a small pail until it thickens. Use more soil than water. Then, carefully mix a leaf or shell into the mud. Make sure it is hidden in the mud.

2 Pour the mixture onto the baking pan.

3 Let the mud dry in sunlight.

4 After the mud has dried, gently break it open. Observe the imprint the object made.

Words to Know

algae: simple living things made up of one or more cells; cells are the basic units of living matter

camouflaged: colored so that animals blend into their surroundings

extinct: no longer alive anywhere on Earth

herds: groups of animals

impression: mark left behind after pressure is applied to an object

mammals: warm-blooded animals that nurse their young

minerals: solid materials found in the natural environment

multi-cellular: made of more than one single unit of plant or animal life

predators: animals that kill and eat other animals

preserved: prevented from decaying or rotting

scavengers: animals that eat dead animals

sediment: material from rocks carried by water, wind, or ice, and left somewhere else

species: a group of similar animals

Index

Log on to www.av2books.com

AV² by Weigl brings you media enhanced books that support active learning. Go to **www.av2books.com**, and enter the special code inside the front cover of this book. You will gain access to enriched and enhanced content that supplements and complements this book. Content includes video, audio, web links, quizzes, a slide show, and activities.

Audio
Listen to sections of
the book read aloud.

Video
Watch informative video clips.

Web Link
Find research sites and
play interactive games.

Try This!
Complete activities and
hands-on experiments.

WHAT'S ONLINE?

 Try This!
Complete activities and
hands-on experiments.

 Web Link
Find research sites and
play interactive games.

 Video
Watch informative
video clips.

 **EXTRA FEATURES**

Pages 6-7 Complete an activity about fossil formation.

Pages 12-13 See if you can identify fossil finds around the world.

Pages 14-15 Use this timeline activity to test your knowledge of world events.

Pages 18-19 Write about a day in the life of a paleontologist.

Page 22 Try the activity in the book, then play an interactive game.

Pages 8-9 Link to more information about amber.

Pages 10-11 Find out more about fossils over time.

Pages 18-19 Learn more about being a paleontologist.

Page 20 Link to facts about fossils.

Pages 4-5 Watch a video about fossils.

Pages 16-17 View a video about paleontology.

 Audio
Hear introductory audio
at the top of every page

Key Words
Study vocabulary, and play
a matching word game.

Slide Show
View images and captions,
and try a writing activity.

AV² Quiz
Take this quiz to test
your knowledge

Due to the dynamic nature of the Internet, some of the URLs and activities provided as part of AV² by Weigl may have changed or ceased to exist. AV² by Weigl accepts no responsibility for any such changes. All media enhanced books are regularly monitored to update addresses and sites in a timely manner. Contact AV² by Weigl at 1-866-649-3445 or av2books@weigl.com with any questions, comments, or feedback.